Van Gogh

HIS LIFE
—AND—
HIS FLOWERS

WENDY L. CIARCI JACKSON

STERLING INNOVATION
An imprint of Sterling Publishing Co., Inc.

New York / London
www.sterlingpublishing.com

STERLING, the Sterling logo, STERLING INNOVATION, and the
Sterling Innovation logo are registered trademarks of Sterling Publishing Co., Inc.

2 4 6 8 10 9 7 5 3 1

Published by Sterling Publishing Co., Inc.
387 Park Avenue South, New York, NY 10016
© 2009 by Wendy L. Ciarci Jackson
Distributed in Canada by Sterling Publishing
c/o Canadian Manda Group, 165 Dufferin Street
Toronto, Ontario, Canada M6K 3H6
Distributed in the United Kingdom by GMC Distribution Services
Castle Place, 166 High Street, Lewes, East Sussex, England BN7 1XU
Distributed in Australia by Capricorn Link (Australia) Pty. Ltd.
P.O. Box 704, Windsor, NSW 2756, Australia

Photo research by Susan Oyama
Designed by Pamela Darcy of Neo9 Design, Inc.

Printed in China
All rights reserved

This book is part of *Van Gogh's Sunflowers In-a-Box* and is not to be sold separately.

Sterling ISBN 978-1-4027-5812-6

For information about custom editions, special sales, premium and
corporate purchases, please contact Sterling Special Sales
Department at 800-805-5489 or specialsales@sterlingpublishing.com.

Contents

—4—
HOW TO BUILD YOUR SUNFLOWERS

—6—
INTRODUCTION

—8—
EARLY LIFE

—14—
EARLY ART, 1880-1886: 227 PAINTINGS

—18—
PARIS, 1886-1888: 221 PAINTINGS

—22—
THE STUDIO OF THE SOUTH, ARLES,
FEBRUARY 1888-MAY 1889: 187 PAINTINGS

—27—
THE SUNFLOWERS

—35—
THE CRISIS

—41—
SAINT-REMY AND AUVERS,
MAY 1889-MAY 1890: 218 PAINTINGS

—44—
VAN GOGH'S LEGACY

—46—
ART CREDITS

—47—
BIBLIOGRAPHY

—48—
INDEX

How to Build Your Sunflowers

Check to make sure you have each of the following items:
- 1 Column Piece (its three panels resemble three giant popsicle sticks cut in half: look for the scalloped edges)
- 1 Vase Piece (this looks like a fan with three panels)
- 1 Vase Lid (perforated circle with three protruding stems)
- 1 Vase Collar (thin band with holes along its midline)
- 6 Sunflowers with pointed petals
- 6 circular Sunflower Centers
- 4 Sunflowers with one hinged edge
- 1 Small Sunflower with one hinged edge
- 8 Stems (four long, two medium, and two short stems)

Punch out the star-shaped piece on the box lid. With your box emptied of its contents, replace the lid.

Expand the Column Piece, holding one side in each hand. Bend at the hinge, bringing the scalloped edges together so that they intertwine. You should now have one tall tube with six sides.

With the scalloped edges pointing down, insert the constructed Column Piece (tube) into the hole in your box lid. Press gently on all sides until the Column is securely in place and has reached the bottom of the box.

Next, expand the Vase Piece. Place the bottom of the Vase Piece over the top of the Column Piece; slide the Vase down the Column until the its base edges meet the box lid and the Column is no longer visible.

Expand the Vase Collar and slide it down the Vase to the Vase's center seam. Fit the holes of the Collar to the corner edges of the Vase in order to secure the Vase at its seams.

Place the Vase Lid on top of the Vase. Secure the lid by expanding the hexagonal bottom piece and fitting it into the Vase/Column. The lid should sit flat against the top of the Vase.

Fold open the six Sunflowers with pointed petals. Place a Sunflower Center in each of these six Sunflowers by fitting the circle into the two curved slits of the Sunflower.

Gather six Stems—the lengths are up to you—and insert them into the vertical slot on the back of each of the six Sunflowers with pointed petals.

Next, gather all of the remaining flowers (four large and one small), and insert each tabbed petal into its corresponding slit to create three-dimensional Sunflowers.

Find the two Sunflowers with hinges that have stem slots on their backs. Insert the two remaining Stems into the slots. Set these aside with your other six pointed-petal Sunflowers.

Slide the remaining three Sunflowers onto the stems protruding from the Vase Lid, using the slit on the back of each.

Now you can arrange your Sunflowers! Insert the eight stemmed Sunflowers into the eight holes in the Vase Lid.

Introduction

What most know, or think they know, about Vincent van Gogh is often exaggerated or blatantly untrue. He is perceived as a violent, antisocial neurotic; an inarticulate peasant with a penchant for prostitutes; a self-taught genius whose visionary talent was due to madness. In fact, Vincent van Gogh was far more compelling, and the facts of his life far more complex. His family, childhood, and early career missteps formed his character and guided him in creating a new art for a new century. The truth of his life does not diminish his accomplishments but instead illuminates his true genius.

Vincent produced over two thousand works in just ten short years—from 1880, when he decided to become an artist, until his death in 1890. He painted his most acclaimed and mature works not in Paris, but in the south of France. There, in the south, he became a painter of sunlight and sunflowers, and yellow dominated his canvases.

In the two short years that he painted there, he completed much of his most famous work, bringing together his interests in surface, color, and composition, creating the foundation for modern art.

THE BEDROOM (1888)

Early Life

Vincent Willem van Gogh was born on March 30, 1853, in the rural village of Groot Zundert, in the Dutch province of North Brabant, near the southern Belgian border, to Anna Carbentus and the Reverend Theodorus van Gogh. He was the second child in his family to be named Vincent; his elder brother Vincent had been stillborn exactly one year earlier. He was the eldest of six children: Anna Cornelia, Theodorus (Theo), Elizabeth Huberta, Wilhemien (Wil) Jacoba, and Cornelius (Cor) Vincent.

While at school, Vincent excelled in languages, including French, German, and English, and he emerged with an appreciation for literature that remained with him throughout his life and became a dominant influence in his art. He was particularly fond of socially conscious writers such as Charles Dickens, William Wordsworth, and the French naturalist writers—including Émile Zola and Victor Hugo. He identified with their sensitive portrayals of peasants and outcasts.

At sixteen, Vincent secured a position with Goupil & Cie, international art dealers with headquarters in Paris. His uncle, also named Vincent, was a partner in the firm. The firm was conservative and showed paintings by established artists sanctioned by the Salon as well as affordable reproductions of the established Dutch, French, Spanish, and Italian masters.

In nineteenth century france, art was controlled by academies and Salons. Academies were institutions under government control and patronage that instructed, fostered, and protected French academic art. They were modeled after the academies of the Italian Renaissance. Societies that engaged in artistic, philosophical, or literary discourse organized by and around a host—but more often a hostess—of standing were called salons (lowercase), while government-sanctioned art exhibitions were called Salons (uppercase). At the top of the hierarchy of Salons and academies was the French Institute, which was (and still is) comprised of five academies, including the Academy of

Fine Arts. The Paris Salon, the official art exhibition of the Academy of Fine Arts, was the most prestigious Salon, but other academies held their own Salons. Innovation was discouraged, and it was nearly impossible to be an independent artist with a new and radical approach.

While working for Goupil & Cie, the young idealistic Vincent began to develop a sense of self, and it was the authoritarian hierarchy of Salons that he eventually rebelled against. Vincent visited museums, attended concerts, read, and sketched. It was also during this time that Vincent started writing to his brother Theo; their correspondence continued for eighteen years and included hundreds of letters later published by Theo's widow.

At nineteen, Vincent was transferred to London. There he developed a serious interest in the Barbizon and Hague Schools of painting, precursors to French Impressionism. The artists of these schools advocated realism. In particular, he was impressed by Jean-Francois Millet's dignified portrayal of peasants and by Gustave Courbet's evocative landscapes. Approaching art much differently than did the Salon artists—who advocated dark, colorless, and slick studio-produced work with historical, mythical, or allegorical themes—Millet and Courbet painted realistic and emotionally sensitive images of common people, ordinary life, and local landscapes. Their subject matter and approach to art influenced Vincent throughout his life.

By all accounts, Vincent was a dedicated clerk who enjoyed London, showing no signs of moody or eccentric behavior until his first fateful encounter with love. While in London, Vincent fell in love with his landlady's daughter—but the girl did not respond in kind and rebuffed his advances. Vincent withdrew from friends and family and lost all interest in his job. The rejection sparked a deep depression in Vincent that would forever resurface during times of emotional turmoil.

After a brief stint in Paris, Vincent returned to England, and taught at two different boarding schools. He began a lifetime habit of sacrifice and penitence through semi-starvation. And his school duties included delivering sermons—something that inspired in him greater religious zeal.

Horrified by his gaunt appearance, Vincent's family again gathered to help. They secured a tutor of Latin and Greek to help him prepare for the theological exam and become a clergyman. But Vincent struggled with his lessons and eventually abandoned his studies; his vision of service to the poor had little in common with the cold intellectualism of organized religion. Vincent could not reconcile passion and intellect, or idealism and realism, and would not submit his will to authority.

Vincent entered a missionary school in Brussels before again dropping out and instead becoming a lay preacher—a post from which he was later dismissed. He was deeply disappointed and felt keenly his series of failures and shortcomings, but remained determined to make something of himself; and so he looked inward to find direction. He believed in the transformative power of literature and art—akin to his own concept of religion. He had a vast knowledge of art and had sketched all his life, and so he decided, at the relatively late age of twenty-seven, to become an artist.

SELF-PORTRAIT (1889)

Early Art
1880-1886: 227 PAINTINGS

Once Vincent decided to become an artist, he pursued it with intensity. He embarked on a disciplined study, though not a traditional one, by first thoroughly learning how to draw, then acquiring sound painting techniques, and lastly by learning color theory. He studied independently with artists, collected prints, and sharpened his eye with

THE POTATO EATERS (1885)

museum visits. In a remarkably short period of time, he mastered the fundamentals and painted his first masterpiece, *The Potato Eaters*.

Vincent traveled to The Hague, where he studied with his cousin by marriage, Anton Mauve, a leader in The Hague School. Vincent became an exceptional draftsman and was adept at using distortion, line, and form to express emotion. In 1882, he learned to paint in watercolor and oil. His paintings during this period were dark and muted, influenced by Rembrandt and the of northern Dutch painting, and contain none of the brilliant colors one finds in his later work. In fact, when Vincent sent work to Theo in Paris he was told that his paintings were too dark and not in line with the current style of Impressionism. Vincent felt the sting of rejection but was determined to advance his art through disciplined study and hard work.

The following November, Vincent moved to Antwerp, only bringing with him *The Potato Eaters*. He embarked on a thorough study of color, with the intent to refine and improve his dark palette. His new paintings expressed his own subjective response to the immediate reality before him through color and brushstroke.

The activities and artistic opportunities of urban life invigorated Vincent. He joined a community of artists and enjoyed critiques and lively artistic debates. He studied the work of established masters Eugene Delacroix, Frans Hals, and Peter Paul Rubens, and was influenced by their quick and rapid brushstrokes as much as by their use of color. He also collected exotic Japanese woodcut prints that decorated his room and increasingly influenced his art.

In addition, Vincent enrolled for the first time in an academy, the École des Beaux-Arts, to work from models and to learn color theory. However, he had already developed a method of working that involved modeling form from the center rather than the contour, and that involved applying paint directly from the tube to the canvas, and his instructors criticized his unorthodox approach—admonishing him to fix his contours and to avoid conveying personal expression with paint. They voted unanimously to demote him, but Vincent, disillusioned with the academy's authoritarian and conservative approach to art, had already quit.

Vincent set out for Paris, confident in his own skills and determined to invigorate his art with a modern sensibility. Here Vincent would find financial and emotional support from Theo and comradery with a community of like-minded artists. In March of 1886, Vincent moved in with Theo, first in Montmartre and later at 54 Rue Lepic.

Paris
1886-1888: 221 PAINTINGS

When Vincent arrived in Paris, Impressionism was already established. Theo showed work by Claude Monet, Camille Pissarro, and Edgar Degas that Vincent viewed firsthand. Monet's paintings in particular emphasized the objective observation of color as well as temperature changes between light and shadow, times of day, and seasons.

Vincent was intrigued by the Impressionists' rapid application of unblended brush strokes, daring compositions, and intense color that paired contrasts of warm and cool and complements such as blue and orange—so much so that he began to incorporate these ideas into his own paintings.

> *The painter of the future will be a colorist such as the world has never seen before.*
>
> (LETTER 482 TO THEO, MAY 4, 1888)

The vanguard during this period was a group of young artists reacting against the Impressionists: Pointillism advocates the use of small dots of complementary colors that blend optically at a distance in order to create a greater vibrancy of color. Vincent was particularly impressed by the Pointillist paintings of Georges-Pierre Seurat and Paul Signac. Seurat had also developed a theory linking emotion to color and to the directional orientation and placement of line above or below the horizon. Cool colors and horizontals clustered below the horizon implied melancholy while warm colors and diagonals clustered above the horizon implied happiness.

Vincent adopted some aspects of Pointillist theory while discarding others. He experimented with the dots of Pointillism for a short time, but the dots became dashes and then strokes with a deliberate direction employed to describe form and to move the viewer's eye around the canvas, as in *Self-Portrait with Felt Hat* (page 20). He eventually developed subjective and spontaneous strokes, but his Paris experiments fine-tuned his sensitivities and paved the way for the work he would execute in Arles.

Vincent participated in exhibitions and referred to his group of friends John Russel, Émile Bernard, Henri de Toulouse-Lautrec, Seurat, and Signac as the artists of the Petit Boulevard, in contrast to the Impressionists of the Grande Boulevard—the formerly avant-garde artists whose work was now fashionable and expensive, such as Monet, Degas, and Pierre-Auguste Renoir.

Vincent's Paris paintings were experimental but not very successful. And yet by the end of his stay,

SELF-PORTRAIT WITH FELT HAT (1887-1888)

Vincent's future artistic direction was clearly evident. He painted with daring and confidence, his work was colorful, his brushstroke pronounced, and his contour emboldened by line. Earlier, he had relied on the subject matter to express sentiment and emotion; in Paris, he turned to color and to his own subjective response to the motif in order to create a new kind of symbolism.

Vincent worked at an incredible pace, creating over two hundred paintings in two years. He also went out on the town with Toulouse-Lautrec, drank absinthe to excess, ate little, smoked much, and, overall, neglected his health. He felt a need to leave Paris. Encouraged by Toulouse-Lautrec's tales of the south of France, Vincent had constructed a romanticized image of the place and became convinced that he would find the right kind of sunlight and the right motifs to take his art to the next level in Arles. Worn out by work, malnutrition, and too much drinking, Vincent left Paris with an utopian dream of creating an art colony, a studio of the south.

The Studio of the South, Arles

FEBRUARY 1888-MAY 1889: 187 PAINTINGS

Vincent painted many of his best-loved works in Arles, where he arrived in February of 1888. He had previously developed a process of improving composition and color through drawings, oil studies, and series, and in Arles he refined his approach. He began to use the Japanese technique of ink and reed to execute drawings and to advance his repertoire of marks. Vincent's process involved finding a subject to his liking, determining the dramatic perspective, completing drawings and studies, and working in a focused series in which he varied the controls of line, shape, and color with each successive painting.

Gradually, Vincent reduced the design of his images to the essentials of bold outline, flattened shape, strong directional brushstrokes, and intense color organized around a limited palette of complementary contrasts. He equated color with music, having taken piano lessons at an earlier time, and he created bright harmonies, forming a new kind of tonal painting that relied on variations of intense but related color with complementary contrast rather than the subtle variations of gray found in traditional tonal works.

In Arles, Vincent studied Seurat's theories and developed a vocabulary that expressed emotion through design and color. His rendering remained true to the subject, but his color became increasingly expressive and unrelated to reality. Vincent's evolving relationship with color, his rendering skills, distilled design sense, and focused process, allowed him to respond spontaneously to the motif and to exaggerate for effect. He was now able to execute emotionally-charged paintings in a single sitting. At last he had found his art.

Vincent was excited with his artwork, and he attributed its highly original expressiveness to the visual qualities of the region. Full of enthusiasm, he wrote to Theo and to his friend, Paul Gauguin, praising the beauty of the women, the quaintness of the town, and the inspirational quality of the countryside. He promoted Arles as an ideal site for an art colony, and asked Gauguin to join him—which Gauguin did, the following year.

Vincent had met Paul Gauguin in November of 1887; Gauguin would become both an artistic inspiration and, later, a catalyst for Vincent's mental decline. Vincent was impressed by Gauguin, a man who, like himself, had begun painting late in life and whose travels, dynamic personality, and physical energy captivated Vincent's romantic imagination. Vincent saw his own youth as time spent in disarray and idleness; Gauguin had sailed the world and had seen firsthand the exotic places that Vincent had only imagined.

At one time, Vincent exchanged two of his sunflower paintings for a single painting by Gauguin. The sunflowers remained among Gauguin's favorites. In this lopsided exchange, one sees Vincent's generosity as well as his deference to Gauguin. The sunflowers, with the pairing of blue and yellow, the flattened shapes, and the emotionally charged brushstrokes that follow form, offer a glimpse into Vincent's future artwork.

FOUR WITHERED SUNFLOWERS (1887)

SUNFLOWERS (1889)

The Sunflowers

If Toulouse-Lautrec is remembered for his dance hall performers and Gauguin for his enigmatic Polynesian women, then Van Gogh is most often associated with his sunflowers. At the same time that he painted portraits, Vincent embarked on a series of sunflower paintings planned as decorations for Gauguin's room. The decorations occupied him until December.

> *You may know that the peony is Jeannin's, the hollyhock belongs to Quost, but the sunflower is mine in a way.*
>
> (LETTER 573 TO THEO, JANUARY 22 OR 23, 1889)

Vincent chose the simple sunflower as a nod to the earlier Paris series that Gauguin admired and to show his friend how far his art had progressed. Originally a native of Peru, the sunflower had long been a symbol in France: first as a religious image of the devoted, turning their faces to God; also as the sun and life-giver; and later as a symbol of love and beauty. This last symbolic affiliation was employed by the aesthetic movement in England, which was spearheaded by Oscar Wilde, a writer with whom Vincent was familiar. For Vincent, sunflowers symbolized gratitude.

Vincent executed paintings of two, three, five, twelve, and fourteen flowers in a vase. He strove to capture the flower's physical and symbolic essence through color and brushstroke. Because they wilted so quickly, Vincent had to paint them in just one sitting, which in turn validated his unorthodox method of quick execution.

Vincent painted by first blocking in the basic composition with line and then establishing color relationships through thinly-applied areas of color. He then built the surface and the color steps (or pitches) that ascended to the most intense hues. At times he applied color directly from the tube or did not thoroughly mix it, so strokes often have multiple veins of color. Working quickly enabled him to be fully

VASE WITH TWELVE SUNFLOWERS (1888)

SUNFLOWERS (1888)

engrossed in the process of painting, as well as engage in a heightened degree of perception and mental focus; he would perceive patterns and translate them directly to the canvas.

In many of his *Sunflowers* (see pages 26 and 30), Vincent used an almost monochromatic color scheme of yellow ocher and yellow, a scheme he had previously employed in a still life of quinces and lemons. The background color is a more intense yellow than the flowers. The singular color scheme produces a feeling of calmness and quiet jubilation, a pleasant happiness rather than frenzied excitement. The brushstroke rhythms in the flower petals and stems create a feeling of alertness. Individual petals are created by individual brushstrokes, and no two areas are painted alike.

Vase with Twelve Sunflowers (page 29) pairs yellow with a light turquoise blue. The background color is applied in short vertical and horizontal strokes and subtly changes color when adjacent to different flowers. The petals are expressive in their shapes and in their linear rhythms. The flower heads turn in a multitude of directions. The color pairing of blue and yellow makes for a quiet but jubilant harmony.

That same year, in September, Vincent completed his series of paintings and is credited as one of the first well-known artists to paint at night from available light. *The Café Terrace on the Place du Forum, Arles, at Night*, combines the familiar yellow and blue of his summer work. The warmth of the yellow and orange gaslight from the café illuminates the entire area. There is a deep perspective that leads the eye down the street to a horse and carriage and

THE CAFÉ TERRACE ON THE PLACE DU FORUM, ARLES, AT NIGHT (1888)

then up into a starry sky. Rhythms abound in the work: in the cobblestone streets, the ellipses of the tables, the linear strokes of the shutters, the patterns of round stars, and in the slashes of lit windows within the dark silhouettes of houses. In the future, Vincent would paint many images with a night sky, the most famous being *Starry Night* (page 43).

In anticipation of Gaugin's arrival, Vincent prepared many decorations for the home they would share including portraits such as that of Mrs. Roulin (*La Berceuse*, or *The Lullaby*); night paintings like that of the Place du Forum; and paintings of landscapes, bridges, public gardens, the interiors of his bedroom, chairs, and a bullfight. The paintings represented the range of Vincent's subject matter and the completely original direction of his color, composition, and brush strokes. He had shed all ties with Impressionism and Neo-Impressionism.

Vincent had high hopes for his collaboration with Gauguin and worked hard to decorate their home and to make it cozy. Vincent repeatedly conceded to Gauguin's ego, flattered his vanity, and deferred to his friend's opinions about art. However, instead of finding gratitude or affirmation of his talent, Vincent was met with Gauguin's criticism. Gauguin disapproved of the disorder in the house, of Vincent's quick and sloppy method of painting—in particular, he disliked finding Vincent's uncapped paint tubes and the heaps of dried, randomly-placed paint on his palette.

The two artists engaged in impassioned discussions, frequently disagreeing. While Vincent listened and at times tried to follow and understand his friend's point of view, Gauguin dismissed many of Vincent's ideas as muddied, illogical ramblings with no intellectual foundation. Already insecure, Vincent began to question himself and his talent. Tension in the house further increased, and Gauguin's repeated threats to leave heightened Vincent's anxiety over the dissolution of his dream to begin an artist's colony.

The Crisis

Vincent worked on his series of decorations for the house from August through December. Sometime in December he envisioned the sunflower paintings as the ends of a triptych with his portrait of Madame Roulin (*La Berceuse;* page 36) in the center. He wanted to create an image that would soothe and comfort, like those brightly-colored religious paintings of saints, akin to the stained glass in churches and cathedrals; Madame Roulin, for Vincent, was a symbol of unconditional motherly love.

    Vincent painted Madame Roulin in Gauguin's ornate chair, like a secular throne, holding a rope attached to a cradle just out of view. Madame Roulin had recently given birth and, at the time, the rope would have been understood as a rocking mechanism for a cradle. He used a strong complementary scheme of red and green with bold outlines and little modeling. The background is a frenzied, flat design of white dahlias, creating strong rhythms and a sense of movement—a startling contrast to the placid figure in the foreground. *La Berceuse*

PORTRAIT OF AUGUSTINE ROULIN, *LA BERCEUSE* (1889)

influenced a younger generation of artists, including Henri Matisse, Pierre Bonnard, and Edouard Vuillard, who appreciated the innovation of its formal design structure as well as Vincent's use of flat areas of color and pattern to create space and mood.

Around the same time, Vincent's behavior became increasingly odd and erratic, and the relationship between Vincent and Gauguin grew more strained. Already notoriously mercurial, his mood now would change suddenly; he would be animated with rapid speech one minute and motionless and silent the next. Gauguin could not bear staying in Arles but was afraid to leave Vincent, ill as he was. Gauguin gave somewhat conflicting accounts of his final days in Arles. He claimed that on numerous occasions, he caught Vincent standing over his bed, silently staring, moved only by a stern command to return to his own room. Another time, the two were drinking absinthe in a café when Vincent violently threw his drink at Gauguin, who then roughly restrained Vincent and led him home where he fell into a deep sleep.

But later, in his memoirs, Gauguin recounted a more infamous series of events that took place on December 23. He wrote that the two had a meal, and that he then immediately left for a walk. He heard the hurried footsteps of Vincent and turned to see him, razor in hand. Gauguin gave his friend a look that caused Vincent to turn immediately for home. Sometime that night, in the yellow house, Vincent cut off the lower portion of his ear, cleaned it, neatly wrapped it in a package, donned a hat, and went to the local brothel where he gave it to a girl named Rachael, telling her to "guard this object carefully" and quickly left.

Vincent had severed an artery and lost a great deal of blood, and he was rushed to a hospital. Gauguin summoned Theo and then left immediately for Paris, without seeing or speaking to Vincent. Vincent was close to death from blood loss, and during his difficult recovery he continued to have fits and hallucinations. Later, after recovering, Vincent had almost no memory of that evening and could not explain what had happened or why—he never did.

For many years, however, Vincent had been plagued by visual and audio hallucinations, as well as by melancholy and an acute sense of failure and guilt—which was likely compounded by Gauguin's departure and his brother's impending marriage. Certainly he was overworked, undernourished, drinking to excess, and isolated. Perhaps all of these conditions, experiences, and emotions combined in his injured mind to precipitate such a self-destructive act.

Vincent remained in the hospital through January of 1889. He did not paint while ill. During his lucid periods, he painted his famous *Self-Portrait with Bandaged Ear and Pipe* (page 40), four copies of *La Berceuse*, and three additional copies of the sunflower paintings.

His physician, Monsiur Rey, insisted that he take better care of himself and blamed his episode on his lifestyle, although Vincent would not give up tobacco or alcohol. Vincent admitted to Theo that in hindsight, his illness had been with him always but had gained in intensity over the summer.

Vincent was at times overcome with emotion and anxiety while working and learned to be careful when summoning the strong sentiments that seemed to trigger an episode. He returned home and tried to pick up the shattered remains of his life and his health, but the townspeople signed a petition to have him committed. This was the final blow for Vincent's self-confidence and his spirit. He voluntarily entered an asylum in Saint-Remy, just fourteen miles from Arles.

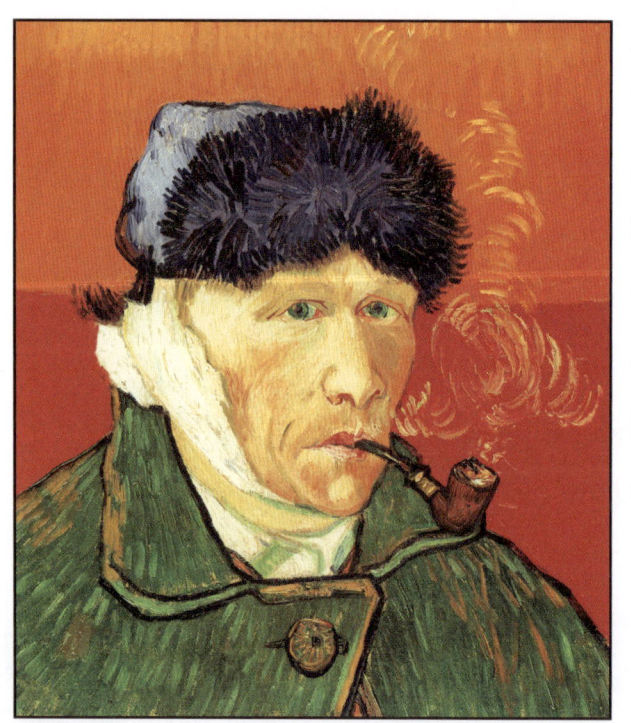

SELF-PORTRAIT WITH BANDAGED EAR AND PIPE (1889)

Saint-Remy and Auvers
MAY 1889–MAY 1890: 218 PAINTINGS

Vincent spent a year in the asylum under a doctor's care and improved his health and his confidence. Vincent stabilized under treatment, but would never be free from his illness.

Vincent executed many paintings in between episodes, though he avoided strong complementary color combinations and instead expressed emotion through swirling strokes of paint. He painted perhaps his most famous painting, *Starry Night*, and his last and most heart wrenching self-portrait during this time.

Starry Night (page 43) combines the familiar pair of blue and yellow. The dominant subdued blue creates a dreamy feeling quite different from his high yellow work of the summer of 1888. The swirling movements of the brushstrokes dominate the painting, and combined with the enigmatic symbolism of the night sky, they hypnotically entrance the viewer. The view is that from his asylum window, but was purportedly painted from memory during the day.

In his *Self-Portrait* (page 13), Vincent seems lost amid the amorphous swirl of paint. His clothes blend with the background atmosphere and his head appears as the only solid structure in the work. His eyes painfully express the effort to retain sanity amidst so much turmoil, and they reveal the painful truth of his tormented soul.

Vincent was invited to participate in two independent art shows in France and one in Belgium, organized by forward-thinking artists in response to the conservative shows of the Academy. Vincent sold a painting at Les XX in Brussels—*Red Vineyard* at Arles—possibly the only one he sold in his lifetime.

Then, on July 27, 1890, Vincent shot himself in a field—but he did not die. He struggled home where his landlord found him and sent for a doctor, who summoned Theo. Vincent seemed on the verge of recovery but died on July 29 with Theo at his side. His funeral was attended by his brother and by fellow artists, and his casket was draped with yellow sunflowers and dahlias.

STARRY NIGHT (1889)

Van Gogh's Legacy

Truth was Vincent's goal in life and in art. Yet the most heartbreaking truth of his life was his suicide. It is tragic that such a good man full of compassion, idealism, passion, and intelligence felt so hopeless that he saw no respite from his illness other than death. Creation and destruction are perhaps two sides of the same coin.

Vincent's mental illness was probably inherited but compounded by overwork, poor nutrition, and abuse of alcohol. Vincent admitted that he had been ill throughout his life and often alluded to a family history of melancholy. There are many theories concerning his mental illness including bipolar disorder, temporal lobe epilepsy, and acute intermittent porphyria, but given the limited understanding of mental illness and the lack of scientific study and information at the time, we may never truly know the nature of his disease.

A paradox, Vincent alienated some individuals and inspired love and devotion in others. He was humble and arrogant. He was often depressed and yet his paintings expressed extreme happiness. He wanted to lift the suffering of others but often created his own. He endured bouts of madness but created lucid art. He adopted the appearance of a simple peasant, but he was an educated and literate man who foresaw the modern direction that art was taking.

Vincent was among the first artists to understand the vital role that self-expression would play in art with a modern sensibility. He was among a new vanguard of artists that dismissed traditional avenues of study and developed their skills according to their own convictions. Within this vanguard, Vincent stood out in his expressive use of color and paint. He paved the way for artists from Picasso to Pollock.

Art Credits

p. 7: © Van Gogh Museum, Amsterdam, The Netherlands / The Bridgeman Art Library

p. 13: © Musée d'Orsay, Paris, France, Giraudon / The Bridgeman Art Library

p. 14: © Van Gogh Museum, Amsterdam, The Netherlands / The Bridgeman Art Library

p. 20: © Van Gogh Museum, Amsterdam, The Netherlands / The Bridgeman Art Library

p. 25: © Rijksmuseum Kroller-Muller, Otterlo, Netherlands / The Bridgeman Art Library

p. 26: © Private Collection / The Bridgeman Art Library

p. 29: © Neue Pinakothek, Munich, Germany / The Bridgeman Art Library

p. 30: © National Gallery, London, UK / The Bridgeman Art Library

p. 32: © Rijksmuseum Kroller-Muller, Otterlo, Netherlands / The Bridgeman Art Library

p. 36: © Private Collection / The Bridgeman Art Library

p. 40: © Private Collection / The Bridgeman Art Library

p. 43: © Museum of Modern Art, New York, USA / The Bridgeman Art Library

Bibliography

Gayford, Martin. *The Yellow House: Van Gogh, Gauguin, and Nine Turbulent weeks in Arles*. New York: Little, Brown and Company, 2006.

Collins, Bradley. *Van Gogh and Gauguin: Electric Arguments and Utopian Dreams*. Cambridge MA: Westview Press, 2001.

Pickvance, Ronald. *Van Gogh in Arles*. New York: The Metropolitan Museum of Art, 1984. An exhibition catalogue.

Walther, Ingo F., Metzger, Rainer. *Vincent Van Gogh: The Complete Paintings, Part I*. Koln: Taschen, 2002. English Translation: Michael Hulse.

Hammacher, A. M. & Renilde. *Van Gogh: A Documentary Biography*. New York: Macmillan Publishing Co., 1982.

Druick, Douglas W., Zegers, Peter Kort, Salvesen, Britt. *Van Gogh and Gauguin: The Studio of the South*. New York: Thames and Hudson, 2001. An exhibition catalogue, The Art Institute of Chicago and The Van Gogh Museum, Amsterdam.

Van Gogh's Letters, unabridged & annotated, http://webexhibits.org/vangogh/, Copyright © 2007 WebExhibits. The letters are Copyright © 2007 RobertHarrison and WebExhibits. All rights reserved.

Van Gogh Museum, Amsterdam, http://www3.vangoghmuseum.nl/vgm/index.jsp?lang=en, Copyright © 2005-2007

The Vincent van Gogh Gallery, http://www.vggallery.com/, Copyright © 1996-2007 David Brooks. All rights reserved.

Index

Academies, 9-10, 16-17
Arles, 22-25, 37. *See also The Café Terrace on the Place du Forum, Arles, at Night* (1888)
The Bedroom (1888), 7
The Café Terrace on the Place du Forum, Arles, at Night (1888), 32-33
Death, of Vincent, 42-43
Ear, cutting off, 38
Early life, 8-13
Family, 8. *See also* Theo
Four Withered Sunflowers (1887), 25
Gauguin, Paul
    joining Vincent, 24
    preparing for arrival of, 27-28, 33-34
    relationship with, 24, 33-34, 37-38
    sunflowers and, 24-25, 27-28
    Vincent's erratic moods and, 37
Health/emotional problems, 35-43, 44-45
    asylum stay and, 40, 41-42
    cutting off ear and, 38
    emotional problems, 37-40
    erratic mood swings, 37
    hospital stay and, 38-39
Impressionism, 10, 15, 18-19, 33
Legacy, of Van Gogh, 6-7, 44-45
Mauve, Anton, 15
Mental health. *See* Health/emotional problems
Paintings. *See also specific paintings*
    1880-1886, 14-17
    1886-1888, 18-21
    1888-1889, 22-25
    1889-1890, 41-43
    finding own style, 22-23
Paris, 18-25
Pointillism, 19
Portrait of Augustine Roulin (*La Berceuse*, 1889), 33, 35-37, 39
The Potato Eaters (1885), 14, 15
Red Vineyard, 42
Roulin, Madame (Mrs.) Augustine, 33, 35-37
Self-Portrait (1889), 41, 42
Self-Portrait with Bandaged Ear and Pipe (1889), 39, 40
Self-Portrait with Felt Hat (1887-1888), 19, 20
Seurat, Georges-Pierre, 19, 20, 23
Starry Night (1889), 33, 41-42, 43
Sunflowers, 26, 27-34
    Four Withered Sunflowers (1887), 25
    Gauguin and, 24-25, 27-28
    painting techniques, 28-31
    Sunflowers (1888), 30
    Sunflowers (1889), 26
    symbolic characteristics, 28
    trading paintings to Gauguin, 24-25
    Vase with Twelve Sunflowers (1888), 29, 31-32
Theo
    art business, 18
    death of Vincent and, 42-43
    letters to, 10, 18, 27
    relationship with, 17
Toulouse-Lautrec, Henri, 20, 21, 27
Vase with Twelve Sunflowers (1888), 29, 31-32